THE
UNICORN
CRAFT BOOK

OVER 25 MAGICAL PROJECTS TO INSPIRE YOUR IMAGINATION

ISABEL URBINA GALLEGO

summersdale

An Hachette UK Company
www.hachette.co.uk

Summersdale Publishers Ltd
Part of Octopus Publishing Group Limited
Carmelite House
50 Victoria Embankment
LONDON
EC4Y 0DZ

www.summersdale.com

Printed and bound in Croatia

ISBN: 978-1-78685-815-3

Substantial discounts on bulk quantities of Summersdale books are available to corporations, professional associations and other organisations. For details contact general enquiries: telephone: +44 (0) 1243 771107 or email: enquiries@summersdale.com.

Disclaimer
Neither the authors nor the publisher can be held responsible for any loss or claim arising out of the use, or misuse, of the suggestions made herein.

Contents

Safety Information

★ It is recommended that all crafts and activities in this book be supervised by an adult.

★ Always take safety precautions when undertaking manual tasks and activities.

★ Always follow the labels of the ingredients and supplies used.

★ Always use your best judgment and do not allow children under the age of three to handle ingredients or small supplies that may be a choking hazard.

★ Adults should handle any chemical products or sharp tools.

Introduction

If this book has reached your hands, surely it's because, like me, you love crafts and unicorns.

Hello, everyone! My name is Isa, and I have created this book with a lot of love especially for you. However, before you start, let me tell you a little more about me.

I have always liked making crafts, but it was three years ago when I decided to share my hobby with the world through my YouTube channels Isa's World (in English) and El Mundo de Isa (in Spanish), where I upload videos every week with tutorials explaining how to make crafts of all styles: kawaii, vintage, country, etc. I also create DIY tutorials for room decorating, organising supplies, crafts for schools and more!

If you haven't heard of or visited my channels, I would be very happy if you visited, especially if you become part of my virtual club with which I love to share this hobby.

Throughout this book you'll notice I have incorporated hashtags so you can showcase your finished projects! When you replicate one of the crafts in this book, upload a photo to any social network with the '#IsasUnicornCrafts' hashtag, so I can see it and give you a like, or comment.

In this book you will discover twenty-seven fun crafts inspired by unicorns, explained step by step, that will awaken your most magical and creative side. You can use the crafts you create to customise a party, organise your school supplies or give as gifts, among many other practical uses.

I hope you enjoy this book as much as I have enjoyed writing it and that through its pages the spirits of unicorns fill your heart with a rainbow of happiness.

BE A UNICORN. LET'S GET STARTED!

IF YOU DON'T HAVE A GREEN
THUMB, IT'S BETTER TO HAVE
PLANTS THAT DON'T NEED
MUCH WATERING.

Unicorn Cactus Pot

#UnicornPot #IsasUnicornCrafts

I love growing plants, but if I'm being honest, even my cactuses dry up. I'm not sure what I'm doing wrong, but for some reason I'm not the best gardener.

I thought that I'd never be able to have a plant on my table, but I didn't let my doubts get the best of me. I needed a solution to my problem, so I thought to myself: *Stones can't dry up!*

I set out on a Sunday morning to create this project, and at the end of the afternoon I had a beautiful unicorn pot on my desk. The difficulty for this project is medium.

SUPPLIES:

- ★ Clay pot
- ★ Acrylic paints (colours: white, light green and dark green)
- ★ Pink and green air-dry modelling clay
- ★ Golden foam paper with glitter
- ★ Super glue
- ★ Black permanent marker
- ★ Soft brush
- ★ Pink chalk
- ★ 4 elongated stones
- ★ 2 small artificial flowers
- ★ Decorative sand (white)

INSTRUCTIONS:

I have chosen a 6-inch/15 cm (diameter) ceramic pot for this project, but this craft does not require exact measurements, so you can choose any size pot that you like.

1   First, paint the pot with white acrylic paint; for better coverage apply two coats of paint, allowing the pot to dry between coats. Let it dry completely. Meanwhile, you can move on to the next step.

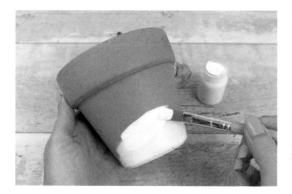

2   Decorate the top rim with some roses. To make the roses, use pink and green modelling clay. Make a bunch of pink balls, about the size of a pea, and crush each with the tip of your finger.

3   Roll the dough with your finger, as shown in the following image. We will call this shape the heart of the rose. Each rose needs a single heart, so make as many as roses as you'd like or fill up the pot's rim entirely.

4 Shape the remaining balls to form drops, then squash them to form the petals. Each rose needs at least fifteen petals. Make sure the petals are different sizes; you'll place the smaller ones in the centre of the rim and the larger ones on the outside.

5 Begin to form the rose. At this point in the process, the petals will be almost dry and won't stick together, so it will be necessary to apply a little water with a brush that will act as glue.

6 Place the petals one by one to form the rose. You can use as many petals as you want; my roses have between twelve and sixteen petals each. To give a touch of green colour, place four or five elongated leaves on the last petal layer.

8 With a black permanent marker, draw the unicorn's eyes. To make your pot's eyes look like mine, they should each have two curved lines with five eyelashes each. Also add some rosy blush on the pot's face. I used pink chalk and applied it with a soft brush.

7 Once the white paint on the pot is dry, continue decorating it. The horn of the unicorn is created by cutting a triangle of gold foam paper with glitter. Depending on the size of your pot and the gold paper foam, the horn should have a height of approximately 3 ¼ inches/7.5 cm. Paste the horn to the pot with a glue that sticks to ceramic. Super glue works well. Then paste five roses that will decorate the front of the unicorn, using the same glue.

9 Look for a few elongated stones that have a smooth surface. Paint them with different shades of green and add a few touches of white to simulate the thorns of a cactus. You can paint polka dots, stripes or crosses so that they look almost like real plants!

10 Finally, decorate the cacti with some artificial fabric flowers. Stick them on the cacti using the same glue from previous steps. To position the cacti inside the pot, fill it with decorative white sand, which you can buy at any plant store.

IF YOU LIKE TO GIVE AWAY THINGS YOU CREATED WITH YOUR OWN HANDS, THIS CRAFT IS A PERFECT GIFT!

YOU DON'T NEED TO KNOW HOW TO DRAW TO CREATE ART!

Unicorn Watercolour Canvas

#UnicornPicture #UnicornDecor #UnicornArt
#UnicornCanvas #IsasUnicornCrafts

I have always liked canvases painted with watercolours, especially those with tons of colours! What I like most is the combination of blue, pink and lilac colours that are so characteristic of unicorns. Recently, I learned an easy trick to create this effect and I'm going to share it with you. It's so easy that you won't even need watercolours.

This project has a low level of difficulty and does not require much work. It will take you less than one hour plus drying time.

SUPPLIES:

★ White canvas
★ Acetate sheet (or similar type of plastic)
★ Paper towels
★ Markers (not permanent) in blue and pink colours
★ Water
★ Sheet of paper
★ Pencil
★ Fine brush
★ PVA glue
★ Blue and silver glitter

INSTRUCTIONS:

1 As I mentioned previously, I'm going to show you a trick to paint watercolour backgrounds using markers. You will need a sheet of acetate (or similar plastic) and paper towels to clean the plastic after each use.

2 Using the markers, add colour to different areas along all the plastic. Do not mix the colours and leave a little separation between the spots.

3 Put drops of water on the canvas. Note: Do not put the drops close together. In the following image, you can see that I am applying the drops of water with a dropper that allows them to come out one by one. However, if you don't have a dropper, don't worry – you can do it with your finger! Just dip the tip of your finger in a glass of water and when you remove it, a drop will remain. Then place the drop on the canvas.

4 Now take the plastic and place it on the canvas so the drops of water and marker ink come into contact with one another. Keep the plastic on the canvas for a few seconds so that the coloured water spots spread out and the canvas absorbs the colours. Then clean the plastic with a paper towel and repeat this process as many times as you want until the entire canvas is full of colour.

5 On a sheet of paper, draw a unicorn silhouette. If you aren't good at drawing, you can find a silhouette on the Internet and print it out. Then cut it out to use it as a template. Place the silhouette on the canvas and trace its outline with a pencil.

6 Next, fill in the silhouette that you just drew with PVA glue. Use a fine brush to avoid getting glue outside of the pencil lines. If some glue spills off the silhouette and onto the canvas, take some cloth and clean it. It is important that only the inside of the silhouette has glue.

7 Sprinkle glitter on the glue. For my unicorn, I decided to put blue glitter on the top and silver on the bottom, but you can use whatever colours you like! Pour the excess glitter onto some paper and save it to use in another project. You will notice that the glitter has stuck to the glue and now the whole silhouette is filled with glitter. Do you love it as much as I do?

8 This canvas can be a great gift for someone special. You can customise it with that person's name. I put my own name because I'm giving it to myself! Repeat the same process as you did with the glitter on the silhouette, only now on the letters of the name. Then let the whole piece dry for two hours.

9 Finally, put some PVA glue on the silhouette and name, covering all areas of glitter. This must be done to protect it, so that the glitter does not detach over time. Don't worry if everything looks white; when it dries, the glue will become transparent.

I'M IN LOVE WITH THIS TECHNIQUE. THIS UNICORN CANVAS LOOKS LIKE A TRUE WORK OF ART.

Unicorn Cork Board

#UnicornBoard #INeedToTakeNotesForImportantThings
#SpiritOfAUnicornButTheMemoryOfAFish #IsasUnicornCrafts

I'm *sooo* excited about this project, guys! I needed a place to put my important notes and I was about to buy a cork board, but they were all so boring. Most were just square boards with a brown wooden frame... definitely not for me! I needed something fun and beautiful, so I thought: *Do it yourself!*

This is one of the easiest crafts you'll find in this book, and it takes very little time to complete. You can likely finish it in less than an hour.

SUPPLIES:

- ★ Pencil
- ★ Cork sheet (¼ inch/6 mm thick)
- ★ Scissors
- ★ Cardboard (¼ inch/6 mm thick)
- ★ PVA glue
- ★ Fine-tipped paint brush
- ★ Acrylic paints (pink and white colours)
- ★ Soft brush
- ★ Foam paper glue
- ★ Pink foam paper
- ★ Double-sided tape to stick on the wall

INSTRUCTIONS:

1 Draw with pencil on the cork a simple outline of a unicorn's profile. I have only drawn the head. It is not necessary to draw details, just the outline will suffice.

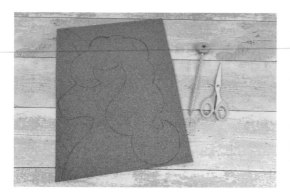

2 Cut out the unicorn's profile using the outside contour as a guide. Cork is a soft material that is easily cut, but do it slowly and carefully. You don't want to crack it!

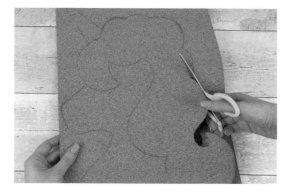

3 Use this figure as a template and trace the outline on cardboard. This cardboard must be at least ¼ inch/6 mm thick, which will give you the necessary depth for adding your tacks and pins.

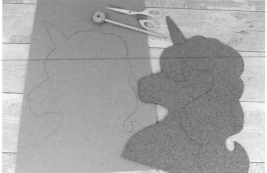

4 Cut out the shape on the cardboard, then glue the cardboard and corkboard together using PVA glue. Make sure that both figures are centred and then place it on a flat surface to dry. The cardboard absorbs moisture from the glue, so it is necessary to place a few heavy books on top of the project while it dries. If no weight is placed on top, it may bend and warp the design.

6 To finish the project, you can paste a super-thin strip of foam paper around the perimeter of the unicorn to give it a more professional look. Use a glue that is appropriate for gluing foam paper.

5 Once the glue is dry, it's time to paint! Choose whichever colour acrylic paints you like. For my corkboard, I painted the unicorn's mane pink and used white on the horn. I decided not to paint the face because I like the contrast between the colours and the cork.

7 If you want to stick your corkboard on the wall, you can use special double-sided tape.

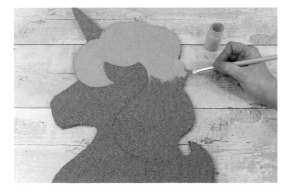

Unicorn Cup

#UnicornCup #ThisCupIsOnlyMine #IsasUnicornCrafts

In my family, I'm known as the 'cup-giver'. They are my weakness. I love having tea in the middle of the afternoon, but I think it tastes better if you drink it in a nice cup. I have tons of mugs and cups, but I was missing a decorated one with an adorable unicorn. This DIY project is easy, but you need the help of an adult because you have to use the oven. It will take approximately three hours to complete.

SUPPLIES:

★ Polymer clay (colours: magenta, white, yellow, beige, blue and purple)
★ Porcelain cup
★ Super glue (or a glue that sticks to porcelain)
★ Modelling clay tools
★ Oven

INSTRUCTIONS:

This time we will use polymer clay. It is a modelling clay that needs to be dried in an oven. Despite this extra step, the result is incredible. We will use this clay because the finished product can then be washed without being damaged, so it is perfect for decorating a cup.

1 First, get a porcelain cup with a smooth surface. Mine will have a unicorn seated on a cupcake. Next, start modelling the base of the cupcake. The polymer clay is a little hard when you first open the package; therefore, you will need to knead it for several minutes until it softens and becomes easier to shape.

2 Take a piece of magenta clay and make a shape like the one you can see in the following image using the modelling tools. This will be the cupcake liner. Position it in its appropriate place on the cup and press a little so that it stays stuck.

3 To make the sponge part of the cake, use a piece of beige clay, make an oval shape (but somewhat irregular), and position it in its appropriate place. Remember to softly press the clay on the cup so that it sticks.

4 Create some details to make it look like a real cupcake: using different colours of clay, add a little white cream on top, some sprinkles and some polka dots on the cupcake liner. Also, make a few lines in the liner to make it more realistic.

5 The picture shows you the white clay shapes that you will need to make the unicorn. In the upper part of the image, you can see the head and the ears. In the lower part, you can see the body, the front legs, and the hind legs. These are very easy to make.

6 Place each piece on the cup to form the unicorn. Add a pair of light pink circles on the hind legs and a beige oval shape that serves as the unicorn's nose.

7 In the next image, you can see some of the details that are shaping this little unicorn. Starting from the top, I have added some small light pink circles to the ears, a small yellow drop that serves as the horn, and an assortment of small colourful clay strands to create the mane. Two small black balls are the unicorn's eyes and two light pink balls can be used as the blush. I used the end of a paintbrush to make the holes for the nostrils. If you keep looking, you'll also notice that I have made a tail using various colours of clay.

8 You can complete your design with a few coloured circles and some candy clouds made with lilac, pink and white clay. When you have finished decorating the cup, it will be time to bake it. Look at the clay's instructions for the temperature and time that the manufacturer recommends. In my case, it indicates thirty minutes at 230ºF/110ºC.

9 When the baking time is over, let the cup cool down. The clay pieces should have hardened with the shape of the cup. These should be easy to remove.

THIS IS A SUPER KAWAII CUP. I LOVE IT!

10 Once you have removed the clay pieces, clean the cup with a dry cloth and apply glue to the back of each piece of clay, then stick them on the cup in their proper places. I used an instant glue that sticks on porcelain. Once it has dried, the cup will be ready to use.

Tip: This cup should not be put in the microwave or in the dishwasher; always handwash with cold water and rub lightly with a soft sponge.

Kawaii Unicorn Frappuccino Handbag

#Unicornfrappuccino #KawaiiHandbag
#UnicornHandbag #IsasUnicornCrafts

Here's how it typically goes when I enter a cafe:

Me: 'Hello! A frappuccino, please.'

Barista: 'Do you want any toppings?'

Me: 'Sure, put a lot of cream, caramel-flavoured syrup, nuts, marshmallows, coloured chips, chocolate chips, a little bit of that edible unicorn glitter. Ah! And one of those decorative umbrellas.'

Barista: 'Are you sure? I think there will hardly be room for your frappuccino.'

Me: 'It doesn't matter, I'd prefer the sweets!'

I love those coffee shops where they have all kinds of sweet drinks. I was inspired by the Unicorn Frappuccino to make this very original handbag. This craft's difficulty level is medium, and it can be completed in approximately three hours.

SUPPLIES:

* Baking paper
* Pencil
* Foam paper (colours: white, black, fuchsia, blue, light pink, turquoise, and three small pieces of yellow, red and lilac)
* Liquid silicone glue (or super glue)
* Blue and pink glitter
* Scissors
* Pink, blue and turquoise markers
* Cotton swabs
* White acrylic paint
* Cord or ribbon to hang the bag

INSTRUCTIONS:

I have designed this animated unicorn frappuccino bag to be in the style of kawaii. It's so adorable with its rosy cheeks! I must warn you that we will use foam paper for this project. Therefore, you will not be able to put much weight in your bag, but you can use it to play or carry things that are not too heavy. With this project, I will teach you a trick to transfer any drawing to foam paper. You will need baking paper; this is a vegetable paper that has a thin wax film on its surface, which makes it ideal for our purposes.

1 Draw the design with a pencil on the baking paper. You can do it all at once or draw each coloured piece separately. In my case, I have decided to draw the outer contour on one sheet and the icing and the details of the cup on another. I think that it's easier this way to transfer the templates to their corresponding colours of foam paper.

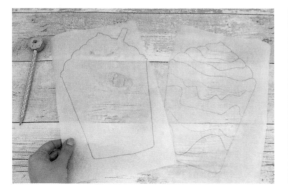

2 Then turn the baking paper over on the foam paper, place each template on top of its corresponding colour (so that the graphite from the pencil is touching the foam paper).Now hold the paper with one hand, keeping it steady. Use something rounded on the lines of the templates to transfer the pencil's graphite to the foam paper. I used the handle of the scissors.

3 When you remove the paper, you will notice that the template has been printed on the foam paper. Now, cut out each piece with the scissors.

4 Next, begin to form the front of the bag. As you can see in the following image, I cut a piece of black foam paper that is the total contour of the drawing. This piece is where you will glue all the others. But before doing this, I will teach you how to shade the coloured pieces; this will add depth to the final product.

6 Next, paste each piece on the black background using liquid silicone glue or super glue. In this case, I have used super glue because it dries instantly.

5 Use markers (not permanent) with colours similar to the pieces of foam paper that you have to shade, except for the white foam paper where we will use blue and pink shading. Colour the entire edge of the foam paper with a line using a marker and then blend it with a cotton swab. You must shade all the pieces. The shading can be underwhelming and may not seem necessary, but when the whole design is formed, it will give the creation depth and a more realistic look.

> **Tip:** Foam paper is a very easy material to cut. However, to make sure that the edges are uniform requires some practice and technique. When cutting foam paper, try to make the cuts of the scissors long and clean. Instead of moving the scissors while cutting, it is better to move the foam paper in curved sections and keep the scissors in the same position.

7 Decorate the cream area with pink and blue glitter. Put glue on the areas you want to decorate and then sprinkle the glitter. Shake off the excess and let it dry. With white acrylic paint, paint a couple of light points inside each eye.

9 To make the bag, cut two foam paper pieces that are 2 ¾ inches/7 cm wide and 15 ¾ inches/40 cm long. Join them together with glue, but leave a gap in the centre of both ends where we will put the cord/string to hang it.

8 To make the back of the bag more resistant, I cut another black outline of the frappuccino and I glued it to the other black outline with super glue to double up. In this step, you must be precise so that both pieces match perfectly.

10 Glue this strip through the lower edge of the bag, leaving a margin of approximately ½ inch/12 mm. Then stick this to the front of the bag. Be precise when placing the back piece to match the front.

Finally, cut a cord strip long enough to hang the bag from your shoulder and stick it inside the hole you left unglued. Use enough glue to make it very strong and let it dry by pressing with your fingers.

I THINK THAT TODAY I WILL WEAR MY NEW BAG WHEN I GO TO MY FAVOURITE CAFE.

Unicorn Galaxy Shoes

#UnicornShoes #UnicornFashion #UnicornStyle
#ILiveInAUniverseOfUnicorns #IsasUnicornCrafts

I think unicorns come from a distant galaxy – a galaxy full of pink, blue and lilac colours, and surely everything is full of glitter. For this project, we will create a unicorn galaxy on our shoes. Be prepared to be looked at and asked a thousand times where you bought these cool shoes.

It's a quick craft to do. It takes approximately two hours plus drying time, and it's also extremely easy. Ready?

SUPPLIES:

- ★ White cloth trainers
- ★ Masking tape
- ★ Blue, pink and white textile paint
- ★ 3 disposable plastic cups
- ★ 2 teaspoons
- ★ Paint sponge
- ★ Toothbrush
- ★ Brush
- ★ Water

INSTRUCTIONS:

You can recycle used white shoes or buy new ones to personalise them.

1 Whatever your choice, first remove the laces and cover the soles with masking tape. Make sure to cover them completely, since any gap can stain them permanently. So, take your time to cover the entire sole and the toe cap, as seen in the image below.

3 With a painting sponge, apply both mixtures you just made to the shoes. Try to combine the colours, but do not mix too much. Clean the sponge with clean water every time you change colour. The goal is to create pink areas and blue areas. Subsequently, lilac areas will appear where both colours mix.

2 The paints need to have a liquid texture so that it's easier to mix the colours. Put a teaspoon of blue paint in a plastic cup, add a little water and stir until you get a thinner texture (be sure not to make it too watery). Do the same with the pink paint.

4 And what is a galaxy without stars? We will create beautiful stars and sparkles with white paint. Scatter small white dots across the backdrop with a fine-tipped paint brush. To create shooting stars, use a toothbrush (the brush you use should no longer be used to brush your teeth; use an old brush for this craft and then keep it with your supplies for other projects). Put white paint on the bristles of the brush and sprinkle the shoes by running your finger over the bristles; you will get splashes similar to the trails of shooting stars. Repeat this a few times for each shoe.

5 With a fine-tipped brush and white paint, draw crosses and full stars. These will be the brightest stars in the galaxy.

YOU ARE DOING SUPER WELL! LET THE SHOES DRY, AND MEANWHILE, WE WILL CONTINUE CUSTOMIZING THE LACES.

6 Place the laces inside a plastic cup and pour in a mixture of pink paint and water until the cords are covered completely. Then, with the help of your brush handle, swish around the cords so that they absorb all the liquid and are soaked with pink! Leave them in the cup for thirty minutes, then spread the laces and shoes out on a plastic sheet. Let them dry outdoors. It will take a whole day to dry, so be patient and do not use them until they have dried completely.

7 If your shoes are already dry, it's time to remove the masking tape. Note that all the areas you covered with the tape are clean and the shoes look new. Use a damp cloth to clean the holes where the laces should be woven, as they are traditionally made of metal and can be easily cleaned.

8 Finally, weave the laces in once they have dried completely. Now you can use your brand new unicorn galaxy shoes! Don't you love them? This craft is a perfect gift for a friend who loves unicorns; just find out their shoe size, and you can make a unique and perfect present.

I'M AFRAID I HAVE SOME NEW FAVOURITE SHOES, AND I'M THINKING THAT MAYBE I CAN CREATE MORE GALAXY-STYLE UNICORN APPAREL WITH THE SAME TECHNIQUE.

Unicorn Headphones

#UnicornHeadphones #There'sALittleUnicornOnMyEar
#IsasUnicornCrafts

I use my headphones daily, but I think they look *soooo* boring. Personalising your headphones is easy and fast; it only takes approximately one hour to do so. However, this type of modelling compound is slow drying, so you will have to wait twenty-four hours to be able to use them.

SUPPLIES:

- ★ Headphones
- ★ Air-dry modelling clay
  (colours: white, pink, blue, yellow and black)
- ★ Super glue
- ★ Toothpick or tool for clay that has a fine tip

INSTRUCTIONS:

I love modelling clay. It is light, easy to work with, air dries, and the pieces stick to each other on contact. We will use this clay to personalise your headphones, so they will look stylish. It will appear as if little unicorns are poking their heads out of your ears! It's cute and fun!

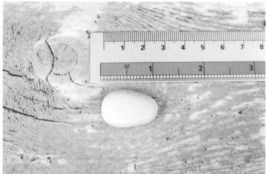

Considering that we are dealing with a pair of headphones, you must make two unicorn heads – one for each ear. My advice is to make them simultaneously. By doing this, it will be easier to keep them consistent, so do everything I explain in the following text twice.

1 Whenever I use a modelling compound, I start by making a ball or sphere. From this, I make all the other shapes that I need. Take a small amount of clay and roll it into a ball, then mould to get a drop shape (as seen in the image). The drop should measure about 1 inch/2.5 cm. This will be the head of the unicorn.

2 Next, you will need a small grey ball. To get this colour, you must mix black and white. Use approximately one tenth of black in proportion to white to create a light grey. Mix the two colours by kneading until you get a uniform colour. Make a small ball, squash it with the tip of your finger, and then place it on the widest part of the head. This will create the nose.

3 Two small grey balls will make up the nostrils. Use a toothpick or a modelling tool that allows you to make the holes in the nostrils; also make a slit on the nose to give each unicorn a smiling mouth.

4 The eyes are very simple to create – just make two small black balls. The blush on the unicorn's cheeks is made with two crushed pink balls on each side of the nose. It's super easy!

5 I think a multicoloured mane will look great, so make a pink strand, a blue strand and a lilac strand (to make the lilac colour, mix blue and pink in equal parts). Place the three strands centred on the head to form the forelock, but try to leave enough space on the sides to place the ears.

6 To form the ears, make two small white balls; you must make a drop shape and place one on each side of the forelock.

7 What distinguishes unicorns from horses is the horn. Well... OK, and magic. But for now, it will be enough for us to add a small horn; notice that it is just a yellow point placed in the centre of the forelock. Remember that this compound is slow drying, so you must wait twenty-four hours before the next step.

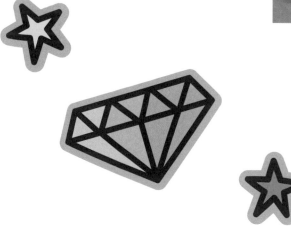

8 After twenty-four hours, our unicorns will have dried and hardened. Now is the time to glue them to the headphones. Be sure to use a glue that works on plastic. Mine is instant drying, so I only used one drop and I waited fifteen seconds.

THESE HEADPHONES LOOK GREAT! I THINK MINE MIGHT EVEN SOUND BETTER NOW. IS THIS MAGIC?

Unicorn Ice-Cream Pen

#UnicornPen #UnicornIceCream #IsasUnicornCrafts

I know, I'm obsessed with everything that looks sweet, but I can't resist! I thought about how I could decorate my pens so that they look fun, and then I thought: *Why not turn them into ice-cream cones?*

The difficulty for this project is medium. To make one pen, you need to do at least one hour of work and let it dry for twenty-four hours.

SUPPLIES:

- ★ Air-dry modelling clay (colours: yellow, white, pink and black)
- ★ Rolling pin and tools for modelling
- ★ Pen
- ★ Scissors
- ★ Coarse salt
- ★ Coloured chalks (your favorite colours)
- ★ Glitter (match the chalk colours above)
- ★ PVA glue
- ★ Liquid silicone glue
- ★ Wooden stick
- ★ Gold acrylic paint
- ★ Pink permanent maker
- ★ Soft brush

INSTRUCTIONS:

Whenever you use modelling clay, it is important that your hands are clean so that residual dirt doesn't get stuck in your mould.

1 Begin by making the waffle cone. Make a yellow clay ball that is approximately the size of a tennis ball. Use a rolling pin to stretch it.

2 Make a cone shape that is as tall as your pen. You can use the scissors to cut the clay. Use a ruler or another flat tool to make lines that form the typical rhombuses in real waffle cones.

Tip: To prevent your cone from warping while it dries, it is better to let it stand on its widest part.

3 Take out the ink tube from the pen and wrap the plastic with the clay cone. Try to make it look like a real ice-cream cone. Remember that this modelling clay sticks to itself on contact, so you only have to join both ends of the cone so that they are fully stuck together. Let it dry for at least five hours.

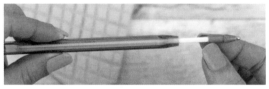

4 To decorate the waffle, we will use salt. However, first you have to give the salt some colour. Put a small amount of coarse salt on paper. Then take the chalk of the colour you like the most and rub it over the salt so that it changes colour. When all the salt has been coloured, mix it with a little glitter of the same colour.

6 Once the PVA glue is dry, it's time to move on to the next step. Put a bit of liquid silicone glue inside the the narrowest part of the cone and insert the pen so that it sticks. Fill the inside of the cone with modelling clay around the pen.

5 Now that the cone has dried enough to maintain its shape, put PVA glue on the cone's opening and rim the cone in the salt/glitter mixture. Let the glue dry. When it is completely dry, it will become transparent.

7 Let's make the ice-cream scoop. Make a white clay ball and place it just above the cone. If the ballpoint sticks out slightly, insert it inside the bottom of the white scoop. Press the ball so that it becomes stuck to the cone.

8 Mould a white clay strand that is the length of the circumference of the ice-cream scoop. Place it around the white ice-cream scoop at the base.

9 To make unicorn ice-cream, it is essential that we have a horn. Use any colour of clay because later we will paint it in a golden colour. Roll a long strand on a wooden stick. The strand should start thicker at one end and decrease in size until it ends in a point. (Please reference the following image.) Then paint the horn with gold-coloured acrylic paint.

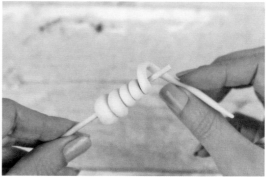

THE ICE-CREAM IS READY; IT SEEMS SO REAL. LET'S TRANSFORM IT INTO UNICORN ICE-CREAM.

10 To make the unicorn's ears, we will mould two white triangles out of clay. Using the permanent marker, make a pink triangle inside of each ear. (You can also use pink paint for this step, if you don't have a permanent marker.)

11 Make several pink clay strands and roll them to form the topping. Stick the topping right on top of the ice-cream scoop. Then, stick the horn on top of the pink cream topping along with one ear on each side of the horn.

12 To finish the project, make a pair of black eyelashes with clay. Place them on the ice-cream scoop and apply a pink chalk blush to each cheek with a soft brush. Then let it dry for twenty-four hours before using it. To avoid the pen becoming warped while it dries, you can put it in a small glass. When it has dried, reinsert the ink mine, and it's ready to write with.

I ASSURE YOU THAT YOU WILL HAVE THE MOST ADORABLE PEN AROUND!

Unicorn Lantern

#UnicornLantern #IlluminatedNights #IsasUnicornCrafts

I will show you how you can make a unicorn lamp from a recycled glass jar. You can place it on your bedside table so that it illuminates your room at night. This lantern is easy to make and fast, although it does take some time to dry. The whole process should take approximately two hours.

SUPPLIES:

★ Glass jar
★ Unicorn silhouette
★ Super glue
★ PVA glue
★ Turquoise glitter
★ Sheet of paper
★ Pink sequined ribbon
★ Artificial flowers
★ Scissors
★ Paint sponge
★ LED candle
★ Hairspray

INSTRUCTIONS:

1 Save an empty glass jar; this craft is made from recycled goods. You will also need the silhouette of a unicorn. You can either make this yourself or search for an image that you like on the internet and print it to use as a template. Make sure the silhouette is smaller than your glass jar. If you decided to print it like I did, cut it out.

2 Then stick the unicorn inside the jar using a glue that sticks to glass. I used super glue that instantly dries. Do not use too much glue; a few drops will be enough.

3 With a paint sponge or a thick brush, spread a generous layer of PVA glue on the outside of the glass jar, excluding the bottom and the area where the lid would go. Don't worry if it looks too white; this type of glue becomes transparent when it dries.

4 Place a clean piece of paper on the table (it will be necessary to catch the excess glitter). Grab the jar by the lip that has no glue and sprinkle turquoise glitter all over the rest of the jar. All the glue must be completely covered with glitter, so recover what falls on the sheet of paper and throw it back on top of the glue. Then let it air dry. Once it's dried, coat the outside of the jar with hairspray so that the glitter does not fall off.

5 Once the hairspray has dried, you can decorate the area where the lid would have gone. Glue a strip of pink sequins around the outline (you can use any glue that sticks on glass). Take several turns until covering the entire thread of the jar.

6 Finally, paste a few artificial flowers to give the lantern a very colourful spring touch. All that remains after that is to put an LED candle inside and to turn it on whenever you want a little bit of magic light.

HOW BEAUTIFUL IS THIS LANTERN?
I LOVE IT BOTH ON AND OFF!

Unicorn Lights Garland

#UnicornGarland #LongLiveTheUnicorns #IsasUnicornCrafts

Who would ever know that this beautiful garland of lights was made with reused plastic cups?

This idea occurred to me when Christmas was over and it was time to remove the Christmas tree. I always keep the lights in a box and put them in the attic until the following year, but this time I wanted to see those beautiful lights all year long. So I recycled the plastic cups from the party the night before and... *presto!* Do you love it? It is an easy craft and it takes about thirty minutes to complete.

SUPPLIES:

- ★ Disposable white plastic cups
- ★ Garland of LED lights (it is important that the bulbs are LED since they do not heat up and thus decreases the risk of a fire)
- ★ Scissors
- ★ Pink and black permanent marker
- ★ Golden cardboard
- ★ Small cloth flowers
- ★ Glue that sticks on plastic
- ★ Pink silk paper
- ★ Transparent tape

INSTRUCTIONS:

To make this garland I have used disposable cups. Use as many cups as light bulbs that you have on your garland of lights. It is better to use a garland that has between ten and twelve bulbs.

1 Cut an X in the bottom of each cup. Through this cut, we will insert the light bulbs, but this will be in the final step. Also, cut off the strip of hard plastic around the rim of the cup.

2 Use permanent markers to draw the unicorn's eyes and blush on each cup. I personally like how closed eyes look, and they are easier to draw than open, so I drew a couple of curved lines with several dashes for eyelashes. The rosy cheeks are two pink spots.

3 Cut out triangles of golden cardboard (mine have glitter because I love everything that shines). These triangles will make up the horns of the unicorns. Paste them on using glue that sticks to the plastic. Also, paste three small artificial flowers at the base of each horn.

4 To give the garland a little variation, some of the cups will be unicorns and others will simply be pink, which will need to be covered with pink silk paper. This type of paper is very thin and will allow light from the bulbs to shine through. Stick it around some of the cups with clear tape.

5 To finish, feed the light bulbs through the Xs that we cut at the beginning of the project. I have alternated using pink and unicorn cups for aesthetic purposes, but feel free to create any combination that you like!

IT'S PERFECT FOR DECORATING A BIRTHDAY PARTY TOO!

MAKE SCHOOL
DAYS MORE FUN!

Unicorn Notebook

#UnicornNotebook #RainbowVomit #FunNotebook
#IsasUnicornCrafts

I finished my school days a few years ago, but I remember that I always decorated some of my notebooks. I especially liked to decorate them when they were newly bought and still had that 'new smell'. I'm not sure how to describe that smell, but I'm sure you know what I mean.

To decorate this notebook, I've been inspired by those apps with filters that recognise your face and transform it into characters that interact with gestures. I especially like the one that makes a rainbow come out of your mouth and gives you big kawaii-style eyes and rosy cheeks. It makes me laugh!

This craft is easy and can be finished in approximately thirty minutes.

SUPPLIES:

★ Notebook
★ Sheet of white cardboard
★ Glue stick
★ White and gold (with glitter) foam paper
★ Liquid silicone glue
★ Pink permanent maker (also you can use pink acrylic paint)
★ Marker pens (colours: black, pink, orange, yellow, blue, green, purple and red)
★ Colourful pompoms
★ Compass
★ Scissors
★ White acrylic paint
★ Pink chalk
★ Soft brush
★ Pencil

INSTRUCTIONS:

It's possible that at this point in the book you've already realised that I love unicorns! That's why my notebook will be a cute kawaii-style unicorn that looks like the rainbow filter on your phone!

I Cut out a sheet of white cardboard to be the same size as the notebook you want to decorate and paste it to the cover with a glue stick.

2 Use white foam paper to make the unicorn's ears and stick them to the notebook with liquid silicone glue. Inside the ears, make some pink triangles to add depth. You can do this with a permanent marker or with pink acrylic paint. The horn of the unicorn is a gold glitter triangle of foam paper; stick it between the two ears also using liquid silicone.

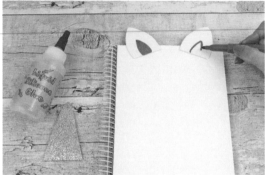

3 To decorate the front of the unicorn, I will use coloured pompoms. These pompoms are very soft, exist in many sizes, and are available in craft stores everywhere. Combine different-coloured pompoms and stick them with liquid silicone.

4 We are going to draw big, round eyes in kawaii style. To make them perfect, use a compass (or a similarly sized round object) and then colour the inside with a black marker. Leave a couple of uncoloured circles inside each eye. This will create the typical shimmer found in kawaii eyes. Use the black marker again to draw a mouth shaped like the number three lying down. Place the mouth between both eyes.

6 Then, paint crosses and dots with white acrylic paint along the entire rainbow. This will create the light flashes. As a final touch, you can paint rosy cheeks with chalk, but be sure to apply it using a soft brush to make it fade.

5 Use coloured markers to draw a rainbow that comes out of the unicorn's mouth. It will be easier to centre if you first trace the lines with a pencil, then colour it with the markers.

WHAT KIND OF UNICORN WOULD IT BE IF IT COULDN'T SNEEZE OUT A RAINBOW?

Unicorn Pencil Case

#UnicornPencilCase #AUnicornAtSchool
#IsasUnicornCrafts

I love to draw. Whenever I have some leisure time, I take my pencil and draw anything that pops into my mind. If I'm being honest, I'm not very good at drawing, but I don't care – I love it.

These days, I can only think of unicorns. Has anyone else noticed this? I drew a unicorn face and it occurred to me that I could transform that drawing into a case to store my pencils. This craft can be completed in one afternoon, in approximately three hours plus the drying time, and has a high level of difficulty.

SUPPLIES:

★ 4 sheets of paper
★ Scissors
★ Masking tape
★ Felt colours (your preference)
★ A magnetic closure for bags
★ Liquid silicone glue

INSTRUCTIONS:

1 The first thing is to draw your own design on a sheet of paper. It is important to anticipate the size of the pencils that you will put inside the case and to make the drawing ¾ inch/2 cm bigger so that the pencils will fit appropriately. Another thing to keep in mind is the part of the drawing that you will use as a cover. For my case, it will be the forelock, so I drew this bigger on my unicorn. If you do not feel inspired to design your own case, you can imitate the one I made while still incorporating elements of your own style.

2 I'm going to teach you how to create your own template. This will help you make different pieces of your case, but also be very useful in making your own templates for other projects. You will need several sheets of paper. The main concept behind creating a template is tracing the separate parts of your drawing individually. If you look at the following image, you can see that I have traced the outline of the face individually on a piece of paper. I have also traced the

horn, eyes, ears and blush. On another sheet of paper, I have traced the different parts of the forelock and the nose. In summary, trace each component individually and cut it out.

3 Stick each piece on its corresponding felt colour with masking tape. This is a trick that I use to avoid having to draw the pieces on the felt and thus not risk getting pencil marks on it. Then cut out the outline with the scissors. Please note that the cream-coloured pieces that correspond to the head and face have a particularity. I will explain how to create them in the next step.

4 I have decided to make the case with a double layer of felt so that it's more robust. It also serves to hide the closure between both layers of felt, but this can be seen more clearly in later steps. As I mentioned previously, the cream-coloured pieces that correspond to the head and face have a particularity that makes them distinguishable from one another. The larger pieces correspond to the back of the case, and have protruding trapezoid shapes at the top (above the unicorn's forelock). This trapezoid is where you are going to stick the forelock. This will also serve as the mechanism where the case will open and close. The smaller cream-coloured face pieces will make up the front of the case. Notice that the bottom contour is the same shape as the back piece, but the top is cut at the base of the ears. I have cut double layers for the unicorn's forelock and its horn, but for the pink zone of the ears, the eyes, the blush and the nose, I have only made single cuts.

5 Now, we begin to form the case. Use liquid silicone to stick it together. First, glue the pieces that make up the back of the case. These are the larger cream-coloured pieces. Next, separately join the pieces that will be the front of the case, leaving the top end open where you will place the magnetic closure. This is so the closure's 'legs' are hidden between both fabrics.

7 Then place both cream-coloured pieces together and join them with a thin line of liquid silicone glue all along the edge of the lower contour, forming the bag that will house the pencils. Be sure to leave the top part open or you won't have anywhere to put the pencils!

6 This kind of closure has two pieces that are joined together by magnets. The pieces each have two 'legs' that must be inserted into the fabric, so make two small cuts in the first layer of felt. Next feed the 'legs' through these cuts and close the inside of the fabric. Join both fabrics with liquid silicone glue.

8 Place the other part of the closure on the piece of the forelock that is in direct contact with the face. Before making the cuts where you should insert the closure, make sure that the forelock are in their correct position so that all the pieces fit together perfectly. Then join both parts of the magnetic closure and adjust this piece of the forelock to its proper position. Pull the trapezoid piece forward and glue the forelock and magnetic closure to it.

9 Then paste on top the other twin piece, hiding the trapezoid and the closure between both pieces of the forelock. Let these pieces dry before continuing. Remember that liquid silicone takes a few minutes to dry, so I recommend putting weight on the case while it dries (I used a heavy book).

10 Once it has dried, remove the weight and paste the rest of the pieces, guiding yourself with your original drawing. Then let it dry and your case will be ready.

Cloud Unicorn
Pencil Holder

#CloudUnicorn #UnicornPencilHolder #IsasUnicornCrafts

I am somewhat disorganised. My table sometimes looks like a flea market for school supplies and the worst thing is that I can never find the pencil that I want to use. I need to get rid of my bad habits. I promise to organise my desk, but for this I need a beautiful pencil holder, so I'll make one myself! Let me think... what if it were... a unicorn cloud?

SUPPLIES:

* ★ Sheet of paper
* ★ Pencil
* ★ Scissors
* ★ Ruler
* ★ Glue
* ★ Thick card (1/10 inch/2.5 mm thick)
* ★ Acrylic paints
* ★ Brush
* ★ Black permanent marker

INSTRUCTIONS:

This pencil holder will be 100 percent your own design. This means that it will be as you imagine it, both in size and shape.

1 We will start by drawing the design on a sheet of paper. In my case, I have chosen a unicorn cloud shape, but take the liberty of drawing whatever you like. Just keep in mind that the base needs to be wide enough keep standing, so do not make circular or pointy shapes in the lower part of the drawing. Or, if you prefer, you can try to imitate my design. It's very easy! As you can see in the following image, I have occupied the entire width of the paper with my drawing, so it will be big enough to hold all my pencils.

2 Take a pair of scissors and cut your drawing around the perimeter. This will be used as a template. Then place your template on the card, hold it with one hand so it does not move, and with a pencil trace the outline on the card. Draw it twice. These identical cut-outs will make up the front and the back of our pencil holder.

3 Cut out both card shapes. This type of card can be somewhat hard, so you will need strong scissors (and possibly the help of an adult).

Tip: To be exact, you can cut leaving a small margin and sand the card with a medium grain sandpaper until you reach the outline of the drawing.

4 Once you have two pieces of card (which should be the same size), outline the areas where you want to divide the pencil holder. First, draw a straight line on the base and then draw some vertical lines that serve as guides for the dividers. For my design, I've divided it into three, which I think is the perfect ratio for my cloud.

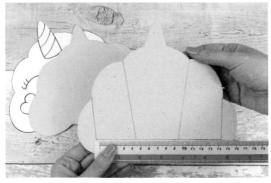

5 Measure the lines you have drawn and cut some pieces of card with those dimensions. In my case, the bottom of each piece is approximately 2 inches/5 cm. Be sure to measure both the height and width! Now cut out each divider and line up each on the pencil line that corresponds to it. Glue them in place (you can use PVA glue or any glue that sticks to cardboard).

THE HARD WORK IS ALMOST DONE!

6 Finally, put glue on each of the edges of the dividers and place the other half of the cloud on top. Try to match the exact position with the back so that when you stand it up, it balances.

8 For my cloud design, I decided to go over all the contours with a black permanent marker so it would be easy for me to paint inside the lines.

7 Add some colour to your design. Start by painting everything white and letting it dry. Then, you can trace with a pencil the rest of the details so it will be much easier to paint.

9 Now that all the contours are drawn with a marker, it is much easier to fill each area with its respective colour. You can use a fine brush to avoid going outside the lines and make sure that your design looks flawless. Notice that I have painted a blue strip around the contour. Adding details are a very nice touch that gives your design depth and character. If you make a mistake and accidentally paint outside of the lines, don't worry: you can always paint over it with white and redo the section. The important thing here is to have fun!

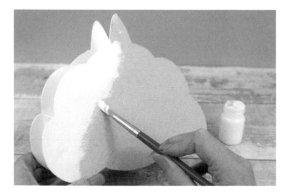

10 Remember that before using the pencil holder, it is necessary to let the paint dry for a few hours. It might be a good idea to let it dry until the next day. And voilá! Don't you think it's amazing that we have created this wonderful pencil holder from a piece of card?

DEAR PENCIL, I WILL NEVER LOSE
SIGHT OF YOU AGAIN.

Unicorn DIY Phone Case

#UnicornPhoneCase #aUnicornOnthePhone #UnicornSelfie
#PhoneCaseDIY #IsasUnicornCrafts

OK, I'm beginning to suspect that I have an obsession with collecting phone cases. I have more than twenty different cases, all of which I made with my own hands. The truth is that what I like most about creating my own phone cases is the time it takes to make the case – and, of course, the selfie in the mirror when it's finished!

In this chapter I will teach you how to customise your phone case(s) in an easy and creative way. For this project, your case will become a unicorn. This craft is relatively easy and will only take you thirty minutes plus drying time.

SUPPLIES:

- ★ Rigid phone case
- ★ Air-dry modelling clay
  (colours: white, fuchsia, yellow, blue and black)
- ★ Rolling pin for kneading
- ★ Ruler
- ★ Scissors
- ★ Liquid silicone glue

INSTRUCTIONS:

1 Take a little fuchsia clay, make a ball about the size of a kiwi (more or less), and flatten it with a rolling pin. You will need to roll a sheet of clay that is approximately ⅕ inch/5 mm thick and is slightly larger than the phone case you are going to decorate.

2 With the help of a ruler, cut the clay as neatly as possible. This cut will be the division between the unicorn's white face and its fuchsia nose, so it must be quite straight. Repeat the same steps you have done so far, but using white clay.

3 Join both colours on the straight edge that you cut with the ruler. The overall sheet of clay must be slightly larger than your phone case.

4 You already know that pieces of clay stick to each other on contact. However, it doesn't stick so well to plastic, so to cover the phone case, it is necessary to apply liquid silicone glue all over the outer surface of the case. Don't forget to apply glue on the sides of the case as well!

5 Then carefully place the case in the centre of the clay sheet, ensuring that the dividing line of both colours is in the centre of the sleeve. Fold up the sides. Then trim off all the excess clay with scissors and soften the edges with your fingers.

6 The cover is now ready to decorate like a unicorn. To make the horn, I have attached three strands of pink, white, and lilac clay (the lilac colour can be obtained by mixing pink clay with blue clay). Then twist the strands as shown in the following image and then cut through the base area with the scissors so that the horn measures approximately 1 ¼ inch/3 cm in height.

7 The rest of the pieces that make up the unicorn's face are very simple to make. Look at the following image: the ears will be formed by two white triangles and two smaller pink triangles. The eyes consist of two black clay ovals and the unicorn's forelock is made up of a variety of multi-coloured clay strands.

'HAVE THE PATIENCE THAT A WISE OLD UNICORN WOULD HAVE.'
OLD UNICORNIAN PROVERB

8 Put each piece in its appropriate place to form the face of the unicorn. Remember that this type of clay sticks to itself on contact; you must be precise. Once they touch, they will not be able to be separated. Finally, mark a shape similar to a 'G' in the area of the nose. You can use the back of a fine brush to do it.

9 Do not forget to hollow out the section where the phone's camera is, as well as the rest of the holes in the case, i.e. charging port, volume controls, etc. You can use small scissors to do this.

Papier-Mâché Unicorn Piggy Bank

#UnicornPiggyBank #UnicornPapierMâché
#IsasUnicornCrafts

P apier-mâché is one of the most-loved techniques in crafts. It is incredible to think that, from paper and glue, you can create beautiful figures. For this project I designed a nice baby unicorn piggy bank where we can keep our coins. This papier-mâché unicorn is easy to make, but requires a lot of drying time (about three days), so make it a weekend project.

SUPPLIES:

- ★ 2 balloons
- ★ Sticky tape
- ★ PVA glue
- ★ Instant glue (super glue)
- ★ Water
- ★ Paper towel
- ★ Newspaper
- ★ Brush
- ★ Scissors
- ★ Pencil
- ★ Black permanent marker
- ★ Silicone or cork stopper
- ★ Acrylic paints: white, blue, pink and yellow

INSTRUCTIONS:

For this papier-mâché piggy bank, the inside needs to be hollow to save the coins. So, we will use balloons as a mould and then remove them when the project is finished.

1 Inflate two balloons and tie them. One balloon must be larger to serve as the mould for the unicorn's body and the other balloon should be smaller to create the head.

2 Join them using sticky tape. Try to place them in the shape of a unicorn. Also, put sticky tape around the conjoining area of the balloons, forming the neck of the unicorn.

3 It's time to make papier-mâché, this technique consists of sticking pieces of paper onto a mould with a mixture of glue and water. After several layers and some drying time, the shell becomes very hard, opening a new world of countless projects.

4 Mix PVA glue and water in a bowl. You should use approximately 70 per cent glue and 30 per cent water. Rip some pieces of paper towel and use a brush to glue them all over the surface of the balloons, being sure to leave no empty spaces. To make it easier to apply, you can use containers to support the balloons while you work. Then let the mould air dry for at least six hours. When those six hours have passed, apply again another layer of paper and let them dry all night.

5 To make the legs, ears, horn, mane and tail of the unicorn, I used newspaper. Form four balls and glue them, using quick glue, to the lower part of the body. These will be the legs. Remember to leave a large gap between the four legs that will be where we will remove the coins later.

6 Repeat the same process to create the horn, the ears, the mane and the tail, and glue them in place. Leave a tiny slit in the head (behind the horn) where you can put your coins. If you prefer, you can do this in the upper part of the body instead.

Tip: It's possible that you have thought to accelerate the drying process with a hairdryer, but this is a serious mistake because the dryer would heat the air inside the balloons, causing them to increase in size so much that they pop and destroy the project or fluctuate back and forth from their normal size between heating and cooling, thus ruining the shape of the papier-mâché. (I'm afraid I learned this from my own experience.)

7 Reapply a new layer of papier-mâché and let it dry until the next day.

8 As a cover for the coin area, you can use a silicone plug or a cork stopper. The one that I used is silicone. I have repurposed it from an empty face-cream jar. You can probably find a jar of cream that carries this type of flexible cap. If you can't find one, you can buy a cork stopper that is approximately 1 ¼ inches/3 cm in diameter. With a pencil, draw the outline of the plug in the lower part of the unicorn's body and trim it with the scissors, then make sure that the plug fits perfectly. Remove the balloons through that hole.

9 Make sure the hole you left on the head or back is large enough to fit the type of coins you'd like to save.

10 Now, it is time for the most fun part of any craft: paint time! Use acrylic paints to bring the piggy bank to life. Paint the body and ears white, the horn and legs yellow, and alternate pink and blue for the mane and tail.

FABULOUS! WITH PAPIER-MÂCHÉ, YOU CAN MAKE MANY GREAT CRAFTS, JUST GIVE FREE REIN TO YOUR IMAGINATION AND CREATE YOUR OWN FIGURES.

IS THERE A BETTER WAY TO DECORATE YOUR ROOM THAN WITH A UNICORN CUSHION?

Unicorn Cushion

#UnicornCushion #MagicDreams #UnicornRoomDecor
#IsasUnicornCrafts

I wanted to decorate my room with things that I made with my own hands and thought I could make a unique cushion to place on my bed. Only, I didn't want the typical boring cushion. I thought to myself: *Why not make a unicorn cushion?* For this project, I'll teach you how to make your own cushion that will make you have magical dreams.

If you're wondering how long it took me to make my cushion, I started on a Saturday morning and it was ready before lunchtime! The difficulty of this craft is medium. As always, when you sew something, it is better to ask for help from someone who has more experience.

SUPPLIES:

★ Microfibre cushion or supersoft microfibre fabric (white)
★ Filling for cushion
★ White thread and needle
★ Felt fabric
(colours: black, yellow, pink, fuchsia, lilac, orange, red and turquoise)
★ Scissors
★ Pencil
★ Paper
★ Liquid silicone glue

INSTRUCTIONS:

To start, you have two options to choose from:

1. You can get a white cushion with supersoft microfibre and customise it. This option is the easiest and you don't need to sew.
2. As a second option, you can make your own cushion, but to do this you have to sew.

In this case, I have chosen option 2 to show you how it's done.

For this option, you will need to purchase supersoft microfibre. If you haven't heard of this, have you seen those incredibly soft sofa blankets? It's that kind of fabric. It can be found in fabric stores or on the internet.

1 On a table, place two equally-sized pieces of cloth, one on top of the other. Make sure they are flat!

2 With a pencil, draw a square on the canvas. Mine is 15 ¾ inches x 15 ¾ inches/40 cm x 40 cm. This size is the most common cushion size, which is why I chose these measurements.

3 Take a needle and some white thread and sew the entire contour of the cushion, just above the pencil mark, but leave a gap to stuff the pillow.

4 You must leave a hole large enough to stuff the pillow with the cushion filling. Turn the fabric inside out and start filling it.

5 Once the pillow is completely stuffed, finish sewing the hole closed. Now, we can go and create the decoration to transform it into a beautiful unicorn cushion.

6 Next, we are going to make the unicorn's ears. To make sure that both ears are the same size, draw an ear shape on a piece of paper (a triangle with two rounded sides). Cut it out to serve as a template. The ears that I have drawn have an approximate height of 4 inches/10 cm and in their widest part 2 ½ inches/6 cm (they are not exact measurements, but it will help you to get an idea for sizing). On a double layer of cloth, trace the ear with your pencil. Remember to make two identical ears.

7 Next, take a needle and some white thread and sew over the pencil mark, leaving the part of the base unsewn.

8 Turn the ears inside out and fill them with stuffing. Insert enough filling so that they are sufficiently stuffed.

9 On pink felt fabric, trace a triangle shape again. Make this template ¼ inch/6 mm smaller than the previous ear template, which should provide enough of a margin to create the inner layer of the ear. Cut out two pink felt pieces using the template and glue one in each ear. You can use liquid silicone glue. Let it dry completely.

10 To make the roses that adorn the mane of this unicorn, we will use all different colours of felt. Cut out several circles, measuring 4 ¾ inches/12 cm in diameter. Next, cut the circle in a spiral. In the following image, you can see that I drew the spiral with a pencil. However, if possible, try to cut the circle without drawing an outline beforehand, so there will be no pencil marks. If you find it difficult, try to make the pencil stroke very light, so it's not too visible.

11 Roll the spiral up, starting from the outside and finishing at the centre of the circle. Use liquid silicone glue to paste the circular shape to the front top centre of the pillow, just below where you will also place the unicorn's horn. Press each for at least thirty seconds so that they are properly glued, and let them dry completely. Repeat the same process with all the circles to form six roses of different colours.

12 On yellow felt, draw a cone with a height of 4 ¾ inches/12 cm. If you want, you can draw it first on a piece of paper and use it as a template. After tracing it on the felt, cut it out.

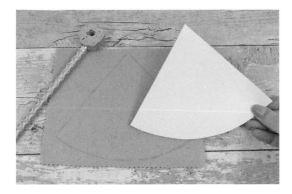

13 Fold the cone in half and sew it along the two straight edges to form the horn. Be sure to leave the top of the cone open. Then fill it with cushion filling, using enough to keep it firm and standing when you glue it to the cushion.

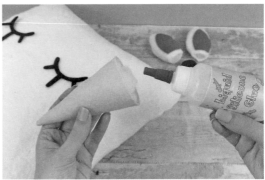

14 To make the eyes, I used black felt. It is very simple, just cut out a curved shape with three tabs for the eyelashes. Now, that we have all the components finished, you just have to stick them with liquid silicone glue.

IT IS FINALLY FINISHED! IT'S *SOO* SOFT... YOU CAN'T STOP HUGGING IT.

Mini Unicorn Piñata

#UnicornPinata #UnicornParty #HappyBirthdayToMe
#InLoveWithSweets #IsasUnicornCrafts

I had never made a piñata prior to writing this book, so I thought that for my first attempt making a small one was better. However, after finishing it, I realised that to make a big one is just as easy. So I think next time I'll do it big. I'm already preparing for my next party!

This is an easy craft, but it's still time consuming. I'm sure it will take you at least an entire afternoon to finish. If you decide to make a giant piñata, it will surely take you a whole day. But the result is incredible!

SUPPLIES:

- ★ Cardboard
- ★ Masking tape
- ★ PVA glue
- ★ Pencil
- ★ Scissors
- ★ Rope
- ★ Crepe paper (colours: white, blue, pink, yellow and purple)
- ★ Coloured card (colours: white, black, light pink, gold with glitter and pink with glitter)
- ★ Sweets (to fill the piñata)

INSTRUCTIONS:

1 You will need two cardboard circles that are approximately 8 inches/20 cm in diameter and a very long strip of cardboard that is 26 inches/65 cm in length and 4 inches/10 cm in width. Roll the long strip up, making sure the lines in the cardboard run horizontally. Find an object with a cylindrical shape and use it to roll the long strip of cardboard.

2 Use masking tape pieces to join the cardboard strip to the contour of one of the circles. Leave the last 4 inches/10 cm free. This will act as the lid for the piñata. Trim any overlap. Then place the other circle on the opposite side and repeat the process.

3 Bend back the 4 inches/10 cm of loose cardboard (the lid) where you will fill the piñata.

4 Like all piñatas, it must be hung so children can hit it and make the sweets fall out. Therefore, you must put a string on it. With the tip of a sharp pencil, pierce the cardboard, making a hole on each side of the lid, then insert a string and knot it on the inside. Once it's been filled with your desired sweets or goodies, seal the piñata with a piece of masking tape.

6 Glue the crepe paper to the piñata using PVA glue. Make sure that all sides of the piñata are completely covered with crepe paper, including the lid.

5 It's time for decorating! As with every project, this is the most fun part! Use crepe paper to decorate the piñata. Take a double-layered strip of white crepe paper about 1⅛ inch/3 cm wide and make vertical cuts with your scissors. Do not cut all the way through the strip. You can use the next image for reference.

7 The unicorn's eyes, ears, blush, and horn will be made with coloured card. The shapes are easy to create: just draw them on the card, cut them out, and then glue them to the piñata using PVA glue.

8 For the horn and the insides of the ears, I used glitter cardboard, which gives the piñata a more glamorous look.

9 The unicorn forelock is also made with coloured crepe paper. Cut it into many strips and stick them around the horn and ears with PVA glue.

AWESOME! IF I REALISED EARLIER IN MY LIFE THAT MAKING A PIÑATA WAS SOOO EASY, I ASSURE YOU THAT I WOULD HAVE MADE ONE FOR EACH ONE OF MY BIRTHDAYS.

Unicorn Cuddly Toy

When I was six years old, I accompanied my older sister Lorena to her friend's house. My sister and her friend were going to do homework together, and I endeavoured to tag along.

When we entered her friend's room, she had a bed full of dolls, and I was impressed. I said, 'Wow, how many dolls do you have?' and I thought that her parents must be millionaires.

Then she knelt at the foot of her bed and pulled out a large box from below. She opened the box and inside there were pieces of cloth, wool, stuffed animals and many colours of yarn. She explained that her mother did not have money to buy dolls, so she made her own dolls out of pieces of clothing that were too small for her.

That experience inspired me to make this beautiful unicorn cuddly toy. To make this, it is necessary to sew, so we can say that this craft is a high level of difficulty. I advise you to ask for help from an adult or someone who may have more experience with sewing.

SUPPLIES:

★ 3 fluffy socks (2 pink and 1 white)
★ Scissors
★ Marker (different colour than the socks)
★ Thread and needle
★ Cushion filling
★ Glossy golden fabric
★ Foam paper (pink glitter and black)
★ Felt fabric (green turquoise, pink and lilac)
★ Liquid silicone glue

INSTRUCTIONS:

1 Get three fluffy socks. The size of your stuffed animal will depend on the size of socks you use; the bigger the sock, the bigger the toy. In the following image, you can see how you have to divide the socks to create the different parts of the unicorn's body. The black lines in the image indicate where to cut and the white dotted lines indicate where to sew.

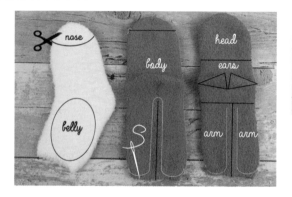

DON'T WORRY IF YOU'RE NOT GOOD AT SEWING. I'M NOT GOOD EITHER, BUT THE FABRIC OF THESE SOCKS WILL HIDE ANY DEFECTS OR MISTAKES IN THE SEAMS!

2 Begin with the body (centre of image). Turn the first fuchsia sock inside out. Looking at the image, draw the dotted line with a marker, so it will be easier to sew. Now, take a needle, thread it, and sew over the line. This is how you will form the unicorn's legs.

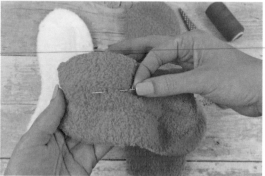

3 Cut along the imaginary straight black line between both legs to separate them. Be careful not to cut the seam that you just made. Also, cut the sock toe along the line indicated in the same diagram on this page. Through that hole, you can turn the sock right-side out.

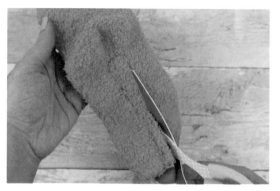

4 In the same way, take the other fuchsia sock and sew the arms. Then, cut the arms and the rest of the pieces as indicated. Follow the lines of the first image to guide you.

5 Fill the body of the unicorn with cushion stuffing until you can't fit any more. The socks' fabric is elastic, so it will increase in size as you introduce the filling and can stretch a considerable amount.

6 It is time to close the body. Use a needle and double thread to sew it. Please note that you will need a resistant thread. Make a very simple zigzag seam. Sew all around the contour until reaching the starting point. Easy, right?

7 Now, pull the strand of thread and you will notice that the fabric has gathered and the hole is closed. Take advantage when the hole is still small and introduce more filling to increase your unicorn's size, then sew the hole from side to side to close it.

8 At this point, you would have ideally sewn and cut the arms from the second sock. For each arm, turn the fabric right-side out so that the seams are inside, stuff the arms with filling and sew the holes closed. Then, sew an arm on each side of the body as seen in the following image, using as much thread as you need to secure the arms.

9 Reference again the first image containing the diagrams. The toe of the second fuchsia sock will be the head of the unicorn. Stuff it with filling and sew it shut, as you did with the body, with double thread and zigzag stitching around the contour. Then sew from side-to-side to close it completely. Once you have your head ready, sew it to the body. Remember: you can use all the thread you want; it is important that the head is firmly fixed to the body.

10 Take the white sock and cut the toe according to the diagram on page 102. This will be the unicorn's nose. Position it on the lower part of the face and sew the whole contour leaving a small hole to stuff it with filling. Once you have filled it in, finish sewing the hole closed.

12 Next, we're going to make the horn. I think many unicorns have a golden horn, so ours should have one too! On a piece of shiny gold cloth, draw a cone shape about 1 ½ inches/4 cm high and cut it using your outline as a guide, leaving a margin of about ⅕ inch/5 mm.

11 With the fabric that you have left over from the second fuchsia sock, cut two triangle shapes to form the ears, sew them (leaving the small end open), and turn the fabric so that the seams stay inside. If necessary, fill them a bit so they stay straight. Then, sew one on each side of the head.

13 Bend the triangle in half so it forms a cone and stitch along the radius you've drawn, leaving a slight overlap. Don't sew the mouth of the cone closed! Next, turn the fabric right-side out and fill the cone with stuffing to form the horn.

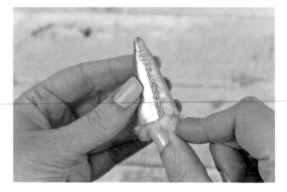

15 To make the eyes, nose and mouth, we will use black and pink glitter foam paper. Cut out the shape of two eyes closed with eyelashes, a pair of pink hearts that will be the nose and a smiling mouth. To stick them to the face you can use liquid silicone glue. I advise you to put a small amount of silicone, so that it looks much cleaner and does not spill out.

14 Now sew the horn right in the centre of the head. Do not worry if you see the seams because will be covered with the unicorn's forelock.

16 To make the unicorn's belly we will cut a piece of the white sock. In this case, you will need an oval shape. Using white thread (so the seam is hidden), sew it on the front of the body.

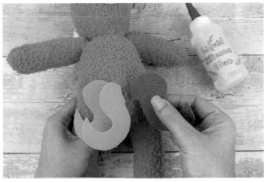

17 For the finishing touches, we need to add the forelock, mane and tail to this beautiful unicorn. We will use felt fabric in a variety of different colours to trace and cut out some undulating shapes. You can imitate the shapes that I used for my unicorn.

19 Now it's ready. You learned how to make your own stuffed unicorn; if you wanted, you could make many unicorns of many different colours and fill your bed with unicorns like my sister's friend with her dolls.

18 Then glue the felt with liquid silicone to your unicorn. Remember to put a nice forelock on the front of the unicorn's head, a healthy mane on the back of its head and a curvy tail on its back. Combine several colours to make it look more beautiful.

A DRINK HOLDER FOR THOSE HOT SUMMER DAYS.

Miniature Unicorn Float Cupholder

#UnicornFloat #UnicornCupHolder #IsasUnicornCrafts

Last summer, I saw these things everywhere. Everyone published photos on Instagram with their beautiful floating unicorn, and I had no choice but to devise a project inspired by this trend.

But, as you know, I feel the need for my crafts to not only be beautiful, but also be useful. So, thinking back to my beach and pool days past, I remembered how many times I spilled my drink on my towel because grass and sand are not the most stable surfaces to rest your drink.

That's why I made this unicorn float that holds your drink. The cupholder is easy to make and will take approximately an hour plus drying time to complete.

SUPPLIES:

- ★ Air-dry modelling clay
  (colours: white, yellow, fuchsia, blue, green, red and grey)
- ★ Glass
- ★ Gold and white acrylic paints
- ★ Black permanent marker
- ★ Transparent acrylic lacquer spray

INSTRUCTIONS:

You already know that an essential part of working with modelling clay is to have very clean hands, since it is a compound where any particles of dirt will stick. For this project, we will use mostly white clay, so before starting, wash and dry your hands.

1 You need a lot of white clay. I used approximately 12 ½ ounces/350 g. Roll a large ball, using the following image as a reference, so it's big enough to occupy the two palms of your hands. I used roughly 10 ½ ounces/300 g of the white clay to make this ball.

2 Model the ball into a doughnut shape with your hands. To do this, lightly squeeze it and push one of your fingers through the centre of the ball to create a hole, then continue modelling and smoothing the surface.

3 The hole in the doughnut has to be large enough to hold a glass, so once you think you have the right measurement, put the doughnut on a table and rest a glass in it. That glass will remain inside the float during the entire drying process.

4 Reserve a small amount of white clay and then make the ears. With the remaining clay, make a thick strand that will make up the neck and head of the unicorn. Make the strand wider at the base and thinner at the top, then fold the top to form the head. Stick the whole piece to the doughnut. Clay sticks on contact, so just touch the pieces together and they will stick.

5 It is time to put the ears on this unicorn. Make small cones of white clay and stick one on each side of the head, leaving enough separation between them to place the horn.

6 The mane and tail of the unicorn must have a variety of colours, so make multi-coloured strands and join them together. Then, with a tool or a ruler, cut them into their respective shapes and stick them to the float.

7 Next, make a cone shape with yellow clay. This will be the horn. Place it between the two ears just before the beginning of the hair, then paint it golden with acrylic paint.

8 Next, make a circle with grey clay that will simulate the inflation valve. You can use the lid of the permanent marker to give it some detail. Then use the black permanent marker to draw a pair of eyes and white acrylic paint to paint a small dot inside each eye.

9 Let the float dry. Unfortunately, the drying process is very slow because the project requires a substantial amount of clay. Remember to place the glass inside the unicorn to maintain its shape and let it dry for three days.

10 Once the clay has dried, apply some varnish acrylic spray and let it dry for as long as the manufacturer recommends. This will protect the cupholder from possible water exposure during the days at the beach or pool. Because of the weight of the clay, your unicorn creation won't actually float in water – but it will be great for keeping your drink steady.

REUSE MATERIALS AND CARE FOR THE ENVIRONMENT.

Unicorn Recycled Desk Organiser

#UnicornOrganiser #It'sSoEasyThatI'mGoingToMake100More
#TakeCareOfTheEnvironment #IsasUnicornCrafts

There is just one thing I like more than doing crafts, and that is doing crafts with recycled materials. I love transforming something that would otherwise be thrown out into a craft project.

It will be very useful to have a place to put my notebooks and papers; a nice unicorn will help me to keep everything organised.

Save a cereal box to transform it into a desk organiser; you can do this in less than an hour, and it's very easy.

SUPPLIES:

- ★ Cereal box
- ★ Pencil
- ★ Ruler
- ★ Scissors
- ★ Acrylic paints
- ★ Brush
- ★ Patterned paper
- ★ Glue stick
- ★ Fabric flower (optional)

INSTRUCTIONS:

1 For this project, we will reuse a cereal box. Most cereals boxes are brightly coloured, but can usually be completely covered with a thick enough paint. It's better to paint the entire box with a light colour. I have chosen very light pink.

2 Once the paint has dried, draw the shape you want your organiser to have using a pencil and a ruler. For mine, I drew a unicorn face on the front and raised the backdrop, but you can make the design however you like! If you choose to use my design, first you must draw the outline of the ears and the horn.

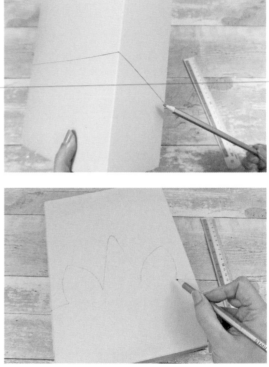

3 For the next step, cut the cardboard box along the pencil line. Take your time to be exact. As my mum always says, 'Hurrying is not a good companion'.

4 Then, break out your acrylic paints and your brush and paint your box to look like a unicorn. I'm going to give my unicorn colourful forelock, closed eyes with big eyelashes, and pink blush on each cheek.

6 As a final touch, I pinned a fabric flower to the unicorn's forelock. It's super cute!

5 Decorate the inside of the box using patterned paper. This type of paper is traditionally used in scrapbooking, so you can find it in any craft store. Choose one that complements the colours you have used to paint the outside of the box. Use a glue stick to paste it to the box.

OK, THIS WAS TOO EASY, BUT IT LOOKS ADORABLE!

KEEP YOUR SECRETS INSIDE THIS MAGIC BOOK.

Unicorn Fantasy Secret Book

#UnicornBook #SecretBook #SecretBox
#IsasUnicornCrafts

Everyone will think it's a fantasy storybook – with magical unicorn stories, castles and princesses. But no one will suspect that it is actually a false book where you can keep your treasures hidden.

This is a medium difficulty craft. We must pay special attention to the measurements of the pieces of cardboard. This is one of the most laborious projects in this book, so you should set aside a weekend for it, since it will take you a couple of days to complete.

SUPPLIES:

* ★ Cardboard (3/16 inch/5 mm)
* ★ Cardboard tube (what's left of a paper towel roll when it's all been used)
* ★ Masking tape
* ★ Glue: liquid silicone, glue stick, PVA glue and super glue
* ★ Fantasy-style image, printed 4 1/3 x 5 1/8 inch/11 cm x 13 cm
* ★ Foil
* ★ White silk paper
* ★ Acrylic paints
* ★ Synthetic moss and some artificial flowers
* ★ Brush
* ★ Pencil
* ★ Water varnish

INSTRUCTIONS:

This craft is a perfect excuse to reuse an old cardboard box. As I've mentioned in previous projects, I love using recycled materials for crafts. Whenever I can, I try to include these materials. For this project, I will use recycled cardboard that is 5 mm thick. In the following image, I have outlined the appropriate measurements in centimetres to be exact. It is important to be precise in this step so that the result looks realistic.

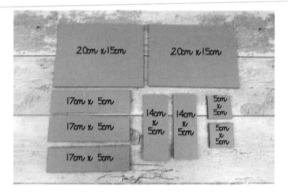

I First, form a rectangle using two 17 x 5 cm pieces of cardboard and the two 14 x 5 cm pieces. Stick them together using liquid silicone glue. Remember that liquid silicone takes a few minutes to dry, so be patient.

2 While these pieces dry, use masking tape to cover the edges of the other cardboard pieces. This will cover the inner ridges of the cardboard so that they are no longer visible. Once the rectangle from the previous step has dried, you should also cover the edges with masking tape.

3 Then paste the first rectangle you made to one of the 20 x 15 cm pieces of cardboard. You must align it with the left edge, and for the rest of the sides there should be 1 cm of overhang left. To glue the cardboard, use liquid silicone glue.

4 Reserve the remaining 20 x 15 cm piece. With the other smaller pieces, form the interior compartments. Glue them with liquid silicone.

5 Use masking tape to create the special hinge that will connect the lid with the rest of the book. This will allow it to open and close with ease. To do this, cut an 18-cm piece of masking tape and use it to join the book to the front of the cover. Position it so that it's level with the base and run your fingers over it several times so that it is firmly stuck in place.

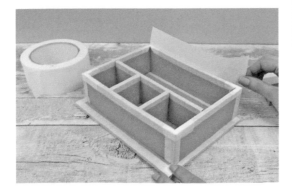

6 Now, open the lid slowly until it forms a 180-degree angle and stick another strip of masking tape inside. Again, pass your fingers over the tape several times so that it adheres well.

7 Surely you have seen an old, robust book containing hundreds of pages with a curved spine? We will give that shape to our book so that it looks more realistic. To create this shape, use a cardboard tube – I used the inside of a paper-towel roll that I reserved once I ran out of paper. Cut the cardboard tube lengthwise and place it on the back of your book to measure how it will fit on the book's spine and mark the appropriate cut marks. Cut the paper-towel roll according to the marks you've made.

8 Place the cardboard tube half just on the edge of the front cover and join it with masking tape. Repeat the same process with the back cover.

9 Find a unicorn image that you like. You can search for it on the internet and print it out, use a cutout from a magazine, or you can even draw it yourself. This image must be approximately 11 cm x 13 cm. Paste it in the centre of the book cover using the glue stick.

10 Use foil to make the raised strands on the front of the book as well as other shapes for aesthetic relief. Foil is great for making 3-D shapes. It sticks with super glue. On the spine of the book, I have made elongated shapes simulating raised bands. Additionally, I have highlighted certain parts, trying to form stones and vegetation. It's not very appealing right now, but when it's finished it will look great.

12 Once the silk paper is dry, it's time to start painting. Use acrylic paints for this project. To unify the colours, apply white as a base colour. Be careful not to paint the image that you pasted on the cover.

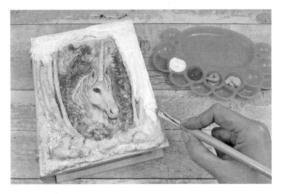

11 In the next step, I will try to unify all the protruding details of the book using white silk paper. To apply the silk paper, you must mix PVA glue with a little water. Make sure the glue maintains its consistency. Cut pieces of silk paper and stick them to the raised details on the front cover. Avoid sticking paper on top of the unicorn image. Once it has dried, stick silk paper on the back cover too and inside the book as well. Do not stick it on the sides. We are trying to add textures, so don't worry if the paper is wrinkled. That is precisely what we need. Keep the book cover open while it dries. This may take two to three hours. Otherwise, if you close it, it may stick, sealing the book shut.

14 Paint the area that simulates the pages of the book with a cream colour; you can also add some lines with grey to make them look like real sheets of paper.

13 I've tried to incorporate the unicorn image colours into the rest of the project, so I used colours like fuchsia, blue, lilac and turquoise. In this step, don't worry too much about the details since the colours are going to mix in this section anyway. Once this has dried, you can be more precise in trying to paint the grey stones and green vegetation. I used several shades of each colour to create a sensation of depth. Also paint the inside of the book and wait for it to dry.

15 To finish the project, stick a bit of synthetic moss between the stones and add some artificial flowers wherever it seems fit. Apply a layer of water varnish to protect the paint. You can apply as a spray or using a brush, depending on your preference.

I LOVE THIS CRAFT. IT'S SO CUTE AND LOOKS LIKE A MAGIC
BOOK WHERE I CAN KEEP MY TREASURES SAFELY HIDDEN.

IS THERE ANYTHING MORE FUN THAN A PYJAMA PARTY?

Unicorn Sleep Mask

#UnicornSleepingEye #UnicornPyjamaParty
#IsasUnicornCrafts

Popcorn, cookies, ice-cream and sleeping on the floor with all your friends can be one of the most fun experiences of your childhood.

This fun do-it-yourself project is the perfect craft to spend the afternoon making with friends before the pyjama party starts. Everyone can make their own sleeping unicorn mask to cover their eyes when it's time for bed. It is an easy craft that can be done in less than two hours.

SUPPLIES:

★ Felt (colours: white, fuchsia, pink, light pink, black, purple and green)
★ Golden fabric
★ Paper
★ Scissors
★ White elastic band
★ Liquid silicone glue
★ Masking tape

Figure 1

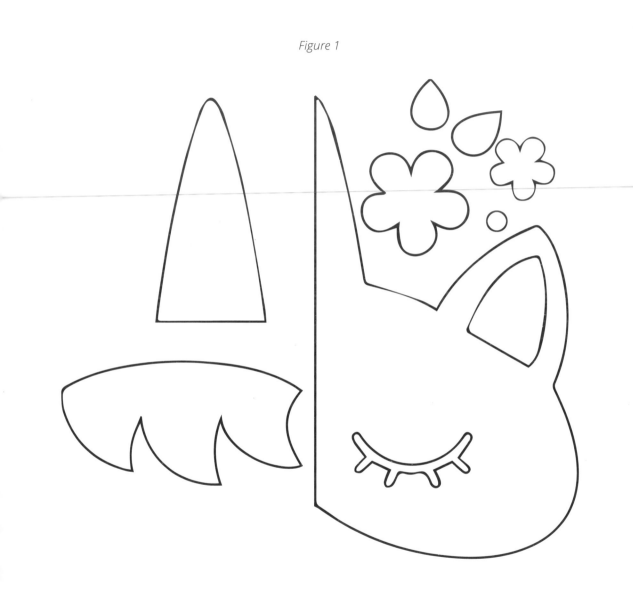

INSTRUCTIONS:

1 Trace the largest part of the template in Figure 1 in the centre of a sheet of paper. Make note that this is only half of the mask.

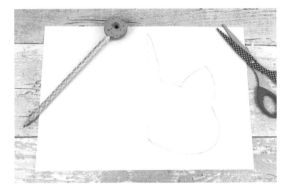

2 Fold the paper along the straight line of the drawing and proceed to cut the outline with the scissors. By doing this, when you unfold the paper, you will have the complete and symmetrical template.

3 Trace and cut out the rest of the pieces from the template so you have all the pieces ready to move on to the next step.

UNICORNS ARE REAL

4 Stick each piece with masking tape onto its corresponding felt colour. Then trim each piece one time, except for the white mask, which you must cut twice. Rather than felt, use shiny golden cloth for the horn.

5 Next, measure the back of your head from one ear to the other and cut a piece of elastic band that is ¾ inch/2 cm smaller than that measurement. Glue it to one of the white mask pieces with liquid silicone glue. Reference the following image for placement.

Tip: Silicone takes more than thirty minutes to dry, so I advise, while drying, to clip the band (and felt) with a clothes pin to hold it in place.

6 Meanwhile, stick the rest of the pieces on the other white felt in the following order: first, stick the golden horn, next the fuchsia forelock, then the green leaves. On the leaves, stick the large piece of the flower, then paste the smaller piece of the flower, and on top, the yellow circle for the flower's centre. Following will be the pink pieces of the ears and then, finally, the eyes.

7 Finally, glue both white pieces together using liquid silicone. Please note that you must leave the ends of the elastic band between them. Now, let it dry at least forty minutes. Before using it, it must be completely dry.

I THINK THIS IS GREAT, BUT THERE'S SOMETHING MISSING... WHO FORGOT TO MAKE POPCORN? IT'S TOTALLY NECESSARY TO FINISH THIS CRAFT!

Unicorn Fluffy Slime

#UnicornSlime #SlimeHomemade #IsasUnicornCrafts

Making homemade slime reminds me of my childhood. There was a time when I wanted to be a scientist and I made my own experiments by mixing kitchen ingredients with toothpaste and hand soap. I thought I would be able to invent something great, but instead the result was a horrible paste.

Luckily, I have now learned a slime recipe that does work. It can be made with simple household ingredients. I'll also show you how to make a unicorn version. Making slime is super easy and it won't take very long. It's also a relaxing craft, so you won't want to stop. I'm sure you'll spend hours playing with this fluffy slime.

SUPPLIES:

- ★ Bowl (large)
- ★ PVA glue
- ★ Acrylic paints
- ★ Spoon (to mix)
- ★ Baking soda
- ★ Shaving cream
- ★ Saline solution for contact lenses

INSTRUCTIONS:

OK this is a lt like a cooking recipe (but it's not edible, so don't put it in your mouth)! Prepare to get a little dirty. Wash your hands before starting and wear older clothes so it doesn't matter if they get stained.

1 In a large bowl, add 4 ⅕ fluid ounces/120 ml of PVA glue with half a teaspoon of whichever colour acrylic paint you like most. Mix until the glue has absorbed the paint colour.

2 Now, add half a teaspoon of baking soda and mix again to incorporate it.

3 Then add shaving cream (about one cup) and mix again. This will make the slime fluffy and pleasant to the touch because the foam causes the glue to fill with air bubbles.

4 Now is the time to turn all this into slime, and the ingredient that will make this possible is saline solution for contact lenses. Add several drops and mix in. You will see that it becomes thick and is hard to remove, but you should keep stirring. Continue adding drops of saline solution until the slime stops sticking to the insides of the bowl.

5 When you're at this point, you can pick it up with your hands and start playing.

6 To create unicorn slime, make this recipe using rainbow colours. You can take pieces of each colour and combine them to make funny unicorn poops.

RELAX BY PLAYING WITH THIS FLUFFY UNICORN SLIME.
WHEN YOU FINISH PLAYING, STORE IT IN A CONTAINER WITH A LID SO IT
DOESN'T DRY OUT AND YOU CAN PLAY WITH IT AGAIN ANOTHER DAY.

Unicorn Story Stones

#UnicornStones #StoryStones #OnceUponATime
#IsasUnicornCrafts

Once upon a time, two brothers were bored on a road trip with their parents. To entertain themselves, they invented games. For example: one game they thought up was to count all the red cars that they saw, or they sang songs from school. However, even those games got boring after a while.

One day, while walking along the beach, they found smooth and flat stones, and they thought of creating a new game to make their car trips more fun.

This craft is easy. Basically, it's going to take the time you need to paint your stones; the more stones you paint, the more time it will take, but your story will ultimately be much longer and more fun.

SUPPLIES:

- ★ Flat and smooth stones (to make painting easier)
- ★ Cloth bag
- ★ Acrylic paints
- ★ Pencil
- ★ Brush
- ★ Black permanent marker

INSTRUCTIONS:

Try to find stones that have a smooth surface and are no bigger than the palm of your hand. You can obtain them from beach areas or on the banks of rivers. Erosion from the water causes the stones to become rounded and smooth.

1 This project requires you to paint stones with different characters, places and objects so you can use them to tell a story. You know I love unicorns, princess stories, castles and magic, so I'll incorporate these ideas into my bag of stones. First, draw on the stone with a pencil your character, place or thing. I started by drawing a unicorn.

2 Now, fill your drawing with white paint. This will make the colours you add at a later stage look much more vivid. Before continuing, you should let the white paint dry. Do this step on several stones at once so that they can all dry simulataneously and decrease your wait time.

3 After a few minutes, once the stones are completely dry, you are ready for the next step. On top of the white paint, redraw with pencil the same design you did at the beginning, including all the details.

4 Then add colour to your drawing with acrylic paints. Use a fine-tipped brush for more precise strokes, since the drawings will likely have some small, intricate details.

5 Wait a few minutes for the paint to dry. Then use a black permanent marker to outline the entire drawing. This includes the smaller details, not just the outline.

6 Get a cloth bag that is big enough to fit all the stones in it. And why not make it prettier? With a pencil, trace a phrase relating to the game. It can be simply 'Story Stones', 'Unicorn Stories', or something a little more detailed, e.g 'Once upon a time...'

7 Now fill in the phrase with black paint; it will give a more sophisticated touch. Then let it dry completely.

8 Reference all the drawings I have made. With these rocks, you could tell many exciting stories. They include everything you'd want in a magical story: a castle, a princess, a spell book, a magical unicorn potion, a frog, a carriage, a magic wand... among many more drawings with which you could form exciting stories.

9 Next, I will explain the rules of the game. If you want, you can write them on paper and insert them into the bag so that all participants can read them.

YEAH, BUT...
HOW DO YOU PLAY?

GAME RULES:

★ Put all the stones in the bag.

★ Give it a good shake.

★ Pick your own way to start your story. I like to use, 'Once upon a time...'

★ Once you start your story, pull out a stone from the bag and put it on the table.

★ Incorporate the drawing from the stone into your story; it should have coherent meaning.

★ Take turns! Pass the bag to the next player. Now they must choose another stone and continue your story with the drawing they pick.

★ Continue until the bag is empty or until the player who started the story says, 'The End'.

SURELY A SUPER-FUN AND POSSIBLY CRAZY STORY WILL BE FORMED!

Unicorn Cake Storage Box

#UnicornCake #UnicornDecor #UnicornGift
#UnicornOrganiser #IsasUnicornCrafts

When I was a child, my mum spent the day yelling 'Isa, clean your room!' I have never been very organised, but now I know why. It's because I didn't have a box as precious as this to organise all my treasures and trinkets.

In the following instructions, I will show you how to decorate a simple cardboard box so that it looks like a unicorn cake. If it was up to me, everything would look like candy and sweets!

Set aside an entire afternoon to make this box. The difficulty is medium because you must take specific measurements of your box so that everything is perfect, but I am sure you will make a great cake!

SUPPLIES:

- ★ Round cardboard box
- ★ Foam paper (colours: white, pink, blue, yellow, purple, fuchsia, black, pink glitter and blue glitter)
- ★ Gold glitter
- ★ Liquid silicone glue
- ★ PVA glue
- ★ Double-sided adhesive tape
- ★ Bond paper
- ★ Yellow air-dry modelling clay
- ★ Gold acrylic paint
- ★ Skewer
- ★ Pink blush
- ★ Brush
- ★ Pencil
- ★ Scissors

INSTRUCTIONS:

Try to get a round and tall cardboard box, my box is approximately 8 inches/ 20 cm high and 7 inches/17 cm in diameter.

1 First, mark with a pencil the place where the lid of the box ends. It is important not to cross into this area so that the box opens and closes without problems.

2 Measure the distance from this mark to the base of the box. You must also measure the circumference of the box and with these measurements cut a piece of foam paper (I have used light blue for my cake). This will be the body of the cake. Glue it onto the box with liquid silicone glue. You must repeat the same procedure with the lid.

3 In the next step, we will make the unicorn's mane. To stick with the cake theme, we should imitate the shapes that a pastry bag makes with buttercream. Therefore, draw the two forms shown in Figure 1 on paper. By doing so, we will form two different sizes.

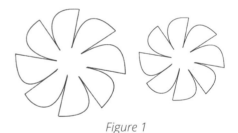

Figure 1

4 Cut out these shapes and use them as a template to trace on foam paper. You will need many of these shapes in various colours. I think the ideal colours for unicorn hair are blue, purple, pink, yellow and fuchsia, but feel free to use whatever colours you like. The box that I made has approximately fifty 'buttercream flowers', so this kept me entertained for quite a while!

5 With the help of the scissors, cut out all the shapes and place a piece of double-sided adhesive tape right in the centre.

6 To simulate the buttercream flower shape, you should stick each tip of the petals in the centre of the flower. Reference the following image for visual aid.

7 Real unicorn cakes have a horn made with fondant. However, in this project, we will use modelling clay to make it. This modelling compound is very similar to fondant, so no one will notice the difference. Take a good amount of clay and stretch it into a very long strand. Make it so it has one pointed end and one thicker end. Roll it into a spiral to form the horn. Once you have formed the horn, stick a thin wooden stick through the bottom (wider side). This will help the horn maintain its shape while it dries. I used a skewer. I'm sure you can find one in your kitchen, but if not, they sell them in most grocery stores or online.

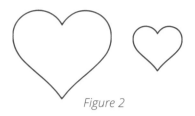

Figure 2

8 To give a chic touch to our cake, add gold acrylic paint and glitter. First, paint the horn with the acrylic paint and let it dry. Then, apply a layer of PVA glue and sprinkle it with gold glitter. Finally, let it dry completely.

10 Using this as a template, you must create two larger hearts using foam paper (I used blue) and two smaller hearts using pink glitter foam paper. Apply liquid silicone glue to stick the small heart in the centre of the big heart as shown. Next, apply a small amount of glue on the bottom of the ear (wide area of the heart) and glue it together to form a three-dimensional unicorn ear.

9 In Figure 2, you can see two hearts – one that's larger and one that's smaller. Take a piece of paper and a pencil, draw the outlines, and cut them out.

11 Now, it's time to assemble all the parts and form the cake. Use liquid silicone glue to stick the horn to the lid. Place the horn closer to the front, rather than exactly in the centre of the lid. The ears should be placed on each side of the horn.

12 It's time to paste the buttercream flowers. Arrange them as if they made up the mane of a unicorn. Place some on the front of the unicorn to form its forelock and then add more to the area behind the horn. You can also place a few on the side to form a 'buttercream flower' waterfall.

13 Do not forget to put eyes on this unicorn. Draw Figure 3 and cut two equal templates (one for the right eye and one for the left), and then use the template to trace and cut two pieces of black foam paper in the shape of closed eyes, then stick them on the cake.

Figure 3

14 To complete the project, decorate the base of the cake using the blue and pink glitter foam paper to form two very long strips. Make one of them ¾ inch/2 cm wide and the other ⅖ inch/1 cm wide. Glue them with liquid silicone around the lower part of the cake.

15 As a final touch, add rosy cheeks. This gives a great kawaii look. You can use pink blush to do so.

Unicorn Headband

#IamAUnicorn #UnicornParty #UnicornSelfie #UnicornHair
#UnicornDance #IsasUnicornCrafts

Create your own unicorn headband and you won't stop taking selfies! This hair accessory is ideal for a unicorn party or to complete a costume. Personally, I would use it for every occasion because I love it! Organise an afternoon of magical crafts with your friends; it will be fun to form a whole unicorn team!

This craft is going to take approximately sixty minutes, and its difficulty is medium because we are going to sew. However, if this part is difficult for you, you can always replace the seam with a line of glue, so there are no excuses. Let's get started!

SUPPLIES:

- ★ Headband (I chose one with a golden cord, but any type will work)
- ★ Pink glitter foam paper
- ★ White felt
- ★ Shiny golden fabric
- ★ Fibre filling
- ★ Artificial flowers
- ★ Slim gold cord
- ★ Thread and needle
- ★ Scissors
- ★ Pencil and paper

INSTRUCTIONS:

Take some paper and a pencil and draw each of the shapes from Figure 1, then cut them out.

Figure 1

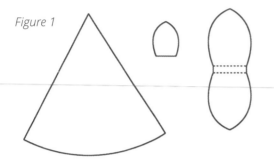

1 Take the golden fabric and the cone-shaped template and cut this shape out of the fabric. You can mark it with a pencil or with masking tape.

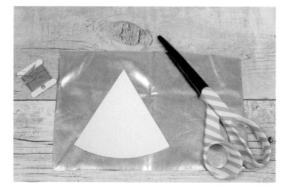

2 Bend the cone in half and thread the needle to sew the straight edge closed. Start sewing just under the tip of the cone.

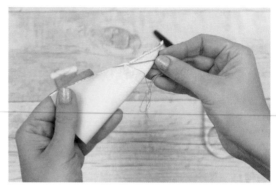

3 If sewing is difficult for you, you can replace the seam with a thin line of glue, but let it dry before continuing. Remember that the shiny gold part should be on the inside. Do not sew or glue the mouth of the cone. Leave this open. Now we must turn the cone inside out, but before this, take the slim golden cord and insert it through the hole we have left at the tip.

4 Tie a knot in the cord and pull it from the tip so the knot is tight inside the cone.

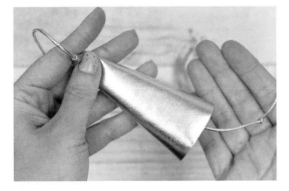

5 In this step, we will stuff the cone with fibre filling. It only requires a little fibre filling, so you can take it from a cushion that you find in your house or use cotton balls.

6 Using the cone as a template, let's draw a felt circle that is the size of the base, then cut out this circle.

7 Apply glue to the inner contour of the cone. Do not add too much, we don't want it to overflow and make a mess.

8 Stick the felt circle to close the cone. Try to keep the circle inside the cone for better results. Let the glue dry for approximately five minutes.

9 Apply a small drop of glue on the tip of the horn and glue the cord so it does not move. Wait for the glue to dry before continuing. Then roll the cord in a spiral down to the base.

10 Glue the cord at the base and cut the surplus.

11 Cut out another felt circle. We will glue the headband between the horn and the felt circle with liquid silicone glue. Make sure that the horn is centred!

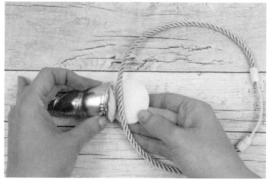

12 Next, use the smallest template to cut out the inner ear shape two times in the foam paper. The medium-sized template will be used to create the outer part of the ears. Using the template, trace the outline twice on white felt and cut out.

13 Place the headband in the centre of the felt ear, apply glue inside and fold it in half so it stays stuck. Then stick the small pink piece in the centre of the ear. Repeat this step on the opposite side of the horn for the other ear.

14 The last step is to add artificial flowers to decorate our headband. Use as many as you want and combine the colours to your preference. Let the glue dry before using the headband.

WELL DONE! OUR UNICORN HEADBAND IS READY! HOW ABOUT A FUNNY PHOTO? SAY 'SELFIIIIEE!'

Unicorn Magic Charm

#UnicornGift #UnicornBFF #UnicornNecklace
#UnicornMagic #IsasUnicornCrafts

Imagine having your own pendant that contains the magic of unicorns. You can also make several of these beautiful charms to give to your best friends!

Seriously, this craft is super easy and super fast. You likely won't spend more than twenty minutes working on it. No, you will not have to go to look for a unicorn to capture its magic; you will only need salt and a few other things.

SUPPLIES:

- ★ Coarse salt
- ★ Paper
- ★ Coloured chalk
- ★ Star-shaped glitter (a few colours)
- ★ Liquid silicone
- ★ Small glass bottles with cork stoppers
- ★ Small screw eyes
- ★ Cord necklace

INSTRUCTIONS:

1 Put a small amount of salt on a piece of paper.

2 Take your chalk and rub it over the salt. Soon you will see the salt change colours to match the chalk!

3 Repeat this step with five different colours. If you want, you can use the same colours as I did. I tried to make it similar to the colours of the rainbow.

4 Using the paper as a funnel, pour a small amount of each coloured salt into your small glass bottle. Ideally, you want to form layers of the same size for each colour. Do not fill it completely, leave some space above to fill it with coloured stars.

6 If you prefer, you can stop here and you will have a beautiful magic charm, or you can turn it into a necklace! For this, you need a small screw eye. Screw it in the centre of the cork and then run a cord or chain through it to hang it from your neck.

5 It is important that the unicorn magic does not escape, so add a little liquid silicone glue and then push in the cork stopper.

I CAN ALREADY FEEL THE MAGIC OF UNICORNS FLOWING.
NOW I AM READY TO ACCOMPLISH ANYTHING!

Conclusion

I hope you have enjoyed your trip through the pages of this book. For me, it has been a pleasure to create these twenty-seven unicorn projects for you. I put a lot of love into each of them.

Remember that 'life looks more beautiful from the back of a unicorn'. This is just a saying to remind you that your imagination has no limits and that you can create anything you set your mind to. Never lose your creative spirit and put passion into everything you do in your life.

Thank you for immersing yourself in these pages and do not forget: Be a unicorn!

With love, Isa ♡

About the Author
Isabel Urbina Gallego (Madrid, Spain)

Isabel has always been a creative person. When she was a child, she spent her leisure time teaching herself how to do handicrafts. In 2014, she decided to turn this hobby into something professional. That's when she created her first YouTube channel called El Mundo de Isa, where, weekly, she teaches her viewers to make beautiful crafts from scratch in Spanish, her native tongue. She teaches crafts for both children and adults and now has a channel in English called Isa's World.

Youtube: www.youtube.com/Mundodeisa and www.youtube.com/c/IsasWorld
Facebook: www.facebook.com/isalunahe
Instagram: www.instagram.com/isalunahe
Twitter: www.twitter.com/isalunahe
Blog: www.elmundodeisa.com

Acknowledgements

This is my first book, and it is the first time that I have embarked on a project like this. I have put all my love into every page and project. I never thought I would have my own book, so this is a dream come true.

I feel so grateful that it is difficult to express this feeling with words. Thanks to all my followers because they are the main component that makes this possible. Isa's World and El Mundo de Isa make me feel so loved with every 'like' and with every comment, always with beautiful phrases that motivate me to continue creating for you. I love each and every one of you. Thanks for being there every time I upload a new video.

To my boyfriend, Victor – my partner, my traveling companion, my love – thank you for believing in all my crazy ideas and for helping me make them become a reality. Thanks for your help and unconditional support both in life and with my job. We make a great team, working hand in hand, and we will always achieve whatever we set out to do. Thanks for taking care of me and for accompanying me. I love you.

To my editor, Jason Schneider, for giving me this opportunity. Without knowing me, you believed in me. Thank you for your trust and for your patience.

To my parents, Teresa and Santiago, first for giving me life and then for always trusting me. You like everything I do, all my ideas seem good, and you never question my decisions. By doing so, you make me feel important. I love you with all my heart. Thank you!

To my sisters – Lorena, Azucena, and Teresa – for valuing my ideas, my opinions, and my work. I know that I can always count on you to make me feel protected like a baby kangaroo tucked in its mother's pouch. Knowing that you are there, I am not afraid of almost anything. Thank you for being my life teachers.

To the rest of my family, to my *Tita* Isabel, to all my nephews, and to my brothers-in-law, because you are there to share my posts, to give them a like, and to contribute your feedback. Thanks for all your support, you are great!

To my other family, that of my boyfriend, Mercedes, Manuel, and Angel, thank you for 'adopting' me and treating me as one more of your own, for integrating me into the family from the first day, and for your help whenever we have needed it. I feel that I have two mums, two dads, and one brother.

Thanks to my two guardian angels, my hairy puppies Arish and Noah, who are inseparable companions that make me happy every morning and fill my heart with joy.

To my friends and colleagues, YouTubers from the WhatsApp group, thank you for your advice and for sharing your experiences. You have been a great help.

And thanks to those of you who are reading this book. Without you, this would not make sense.

Have you enjoyed this book?

If so, why not write a review on your favourite website?

If you're interested in finding out more about our books,
find us on Facebook at **Summersdale Publishers** and
follow us on Twitter at **@Summersdale**.

Thanks very much for buying this Summersdale book.

www.summersdale.com